A Child's Dream

by

The Children of St Peter's Methodist Primary School, Canterbury

and

The Dean of Canterbury, The Very Reverend Dr Robert Willis

The Mayor of Canterbury, George Metcalfe

with Brian Moses, John Rice and Dan Simpson

Foreword by The Right Reverend Trevor Willmott, Bishop of Dover

Edited by Sue Hunt and Michelle Crowther

Illustrated by Ed Hunt and Sofiah Garrard

Contents

This book is dedicated to the memory of three young peacemakers

Jacob Barnes, Lucy Steel, and John Livett

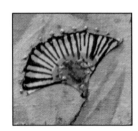

Contributors

The Dean of Canterbury, The Very Reverend Dr Robert Willis

The Mayor of Canterbury, George Metcalfe

Brian Moses - Poet

John Rice - Poet

Dan Simpson - Poet

Sue Hunt - Librarian

Michelle Crowther – Parent

Sofiah Garrard - Artist

The Children of St Peter's Methodist Primary School, Canterbury

Year 6: James Richardson, Luka Thomson, Maria Fox, Noah Stephens, Niko Hodges, Adam Brook, Calvin Lewis, Zach Hill, Charlotte Bates

Year 5: Pascal Sleigh, Rachel Garrett

Year 4: Henry Crowther, Alex Richardson

Year 3: Anoushka Roy, Iliana Roy, Clement Thurston, Serafina Harper

Year 2: Mia Cornfoot, Elsa Lazara-Fitzgerald, Nicholas Smiley

Year 1: Manny Sleigh, Catriona Rowlands, Carlos Almodovar White

Foreword

"Blessed are the peacemakers, for they shall be called the children of God".

What, I wonder, do you think is the most important aspect of a child's education? For me, the answer is simple: to give attention to all aspects of a child's person and to help every child to know and experience the joy of being a beloved child of God.

St Peter's Methodist Primary School is founded on a set of values – values which every member of the school seeks to live out in the daily round of activities.

These poems capture one of these such values – Peace. In the chaos and uncertainties of today's world, being a Peacemaker is both a costly and demanding calling.

As you read these uplifting and challenging poems I hope, with me, you too will be encouraged to play your part in helping to build God's Kingdom of Peace and Justice.

The Right Reverend Trevor Willmott, Bishop of Dover

A Child's Dream of Peace

From the haunting of hatred,

From the terrors of night,

From fire and the sword,

We can float to the light,

On a child's dream of peace.

Sue Hunt

The Quest for the Blue Bird

The Quest for the Blue Bird

One Sunday afternoon, Anoushka, Iliana, Clement and Mahmud, decide to visit the British Museum. In the Egyptian gallery they meet a grey-haired, bespectacled curator holding a broken blue amulet and sighing. Muttering, he warns them that there will never be peace in Europe unless a bluebird guards the ancient artefacts of the British Museum.

The children set off on an adventure to find the bird and restore peace. They borrow a magical hot air balloon from Mahmud's uncle and float across Europe. They cross France and Italy, travelling further and further back in time, until they reach Ancient Egypt. Here are their adventures...

The hot air balloon takes the children through space and time.

In my Warm Leather Hat

In my warm leather hat and flying goggles,

The cool wind is like gentle fingers on my cheek.

White clouds as fluffy as a poodle, newly washed;

The fiery sun like a shiny gold coin, dazzles me,

Teasing my eyelashes.

In my lonely bubble I can hear a brass band tooting,

A fierce dog barking, a school bell ringing.

The burning fire reminds me of summer bonfires on the beach.

My carriage in the sky takes me where I long to be:

To the shore at sunset, listening to the crashing waves,

To the colourful city of sweet smells,

To the magical land of enchanted castles.

Mia Cornfoot, Elsa Lazara-Fitzgerald, Nicholas Smiley – Year 2

The children fly in the hot air balloon over Kent. It is 1945 and war rages across Europe.

There'll Be Bluebirds

The skies are leaden with monstrous craft,

Dogfight trails,

The rat-a-tat-tat of gun fire.

Our childhoods stolen by an argument,

We do not understand.

We dream of playing in the streets,

Of tag and kiss chase.

No more air raid shelters,

Or bomb sites,

Or eerie sirens,

The radio crackles,

Lumping bad news with songs of hope.

We dream of tomorrow,

The warm embrace of loved ones,

We dream of peace.

Michelle Crowther

Floating over France, the children witness the Battle of Agincourt taking place. They have travelled back to 1415.

Agincourt

Heavy blankets of rain pour down on our balloon,

Like soldiers sieging a fortress.

Below the dark grey clouds,

A vibrant sea of silver, red and black -

The pennants, shields and armour,

Of a monstrous battle.

The foot men move forward, screening the nobles,

Like pawns in a desperate game of chess.

The horses charge until they sink in the treacle-like mud,

The slaughterhouse screams of dying men,

As waves of arrows rain down on a thousand silvery stars.

A world turned upside-down.

I see no blue bird here, no lark, no dove,

Only blotches of bright red blood growing like irritated skin.

James Richardson, Luka Thompson, Maria Fox, Noah Stephens and Niko Hodges – Year 6

Travelling further back in time, the children see Hannibal leading an army to war across the Alps

Hannibal

Below us, a thread of soldiers
Is woven onto the mountain pass,
Their helmets glittering, like golden stitches.

Marching boots whisper their dreadful secret,
Disturbing the song of the snow finch,
In its nest.

We look for the bluebird,
Hoping to find peace,
Among the craggy peaks.

But see the mighty elephants –
A terror-column of grey and gold
As Hannibal leads on.

Michelle Crowther with inspiration from Class 6

The children arrive in Ancient Egypt, a land of Pharaohs and pyramids.

Egypt

Drifting in our hot air balloon,

High, above the Pyramids of Giza,

Sand dusting our eyelashes,

We crash into the Sphinx

Which is taller than any giraffe in any zoo.

Frantically steadying the basket,

We rock like a baby in an unsteady cradle.

"Scaredy cat! Scaredy cat, sitting on the door mat!"

It's as hot as an oven,

Burning me like the pan I once touched

When mother said, "No!"

We are on our quest for the blue bird.

Happy to be wearing shorts and summer dresses,

The soft wind brushing against our bare arms.

Glinting, we see in the desert sand

An ancient amulet - Anubis's treasure from another age.

Can it be the blue bird we are seeking?

Anoushka Roy, Iliana Roy, and Clement Thurston – Year 3

The bluebird is found among the pyramids and the children can return.

The Bluebird

Staggering through the fiery furnace of Egypt,

The blistering sand on our feet,

Edging towards the amulet,

Hypnotizing and still,

Glinting.

Cool,

Shiny and blue,

A relief from the burning climate,

The bluebird of peace, soothing in our hands,

Spreads its wings.

Adam Brook, Pascal Sleigh, Rachel Garrett - Year 6

Protected by the magical blue bird, the children float across thirteenth century Italy.

Assisi

The lightness of the air

Strangely warm,

Urging us on.

Below we see a boy,

With a basket of doves.

A rush of feathery wings,

A torrent of birds

Soaring, Dizzying

Joining us in our quest,

Released by a friendly stranger.

Rachel Garrett and Pascal Sleigh - Year 5

Nearly home, the children witness scenes of peace on the battlefields of World War I.

The Christmas Truce

A man emerged from the German trench,

A battered leather ball at his feet,

Clad in his green uniform, no gun in his hand,

A tiny ant in the frosty field,

Treks over to the trench of his foes,

Inviting them up to play.

Suddenly a mere eleven Englishmen came up

Over the lip of the trenches,

Firearms absent,

Mirrored actions from the German side,

And play started.

More soldiers come up,

Greeting their foes like friends,

Exchanging photos and cigarettes.

What a glorious moment,

Harmony amidst a war.

Adam Brook and James Richardson - Year 6

The children tired, but happy, dream of home.

Standing on Air

Standing on air, dizzy and high

Off through the clouds, we float in the sky,

Sleepy in our peaceful bubble,

Fire crackle wakes us.

In the quiet, we hear the whisper of the lonely wind.

The faraway Earth drifts slowly past.

Beneath us, tiny trees wave to us,

The bright light dazzles us, the sun surprises us.

Our magical balloon takes us where we long to be:

A rainy city full of wandering deer,

A sunny hot garden with a tree to climb,

Granny's house full of secret cupboards,

- Home.

Manny Sleigh, Catriona Rowlands, Carlos Almodovar White – Year 1

The Children Return

The children arrive home with the amulet, their hot air balloon bumping down in Mahmud's garden. Racing across London, they take the bluebird to the British museum to the delight of the curator.

Peace is declared in Europe and the Prime Minister, Winston Churchill thanks brave Anoushka, Iliana, Clement and Mahmud for undertaking their dangerous mission. Shaking hands with the children outside Number 10, Downing Street, he congratulates them.

 "You all came back safely!" he cried, "And not even a broken ankle!"

The British Museum

They held the bluebird tight

The curator sighed with joy

And placed it upon a pedestal

Where it gleamed in the sunlit gallery.

Gunshot stopped,

The bird shimmered

A world once more at peace.

Calvin Lewis, Zach Hill - Year 6

Poems of Peace

Angel of Peace

Like pure white light,

Like a prism that glows,

The angel of peace is dressed in many colours.

As I walk in her magical garden

The seasons blend.

Red roses fill me with sleepy warmth.

Treading through deep blue violets and forget-me-nots

Is like paddling in a calm summer sea

Waving at a tiny hot air balloon high in the sky.

I smell the fresh green scent of trees waking in the Spring

And I feel safe and still.

At the day's end the sun sets, butter yellow and raspberry ice cream pink.

Soon I will be tucked up in a bed

As soft as angel's wings.

Serafina Harper - Class 3 and Charlotte Bates - Class 6

Peace

Peace is a gift when all sleep sound
    After a happy day
When none have cried and none have frowned
    At meals or work or play.

Peace is a time when life is good
    And no-one is afraid
When all feel free to be themselves
    And happy plans are made.

Peace is a place where all feel safe
    Where gifts and skills are used,
Where plants and creatures, life and love
    Are treasured not abused.

Peace is a hope, a vision bright
    We have for all the earth,
That all may rise and face the light
    And greet each new day's birth

The Very Reverend Dr Robert Willis

Dean of Canterbury

I Can See a Boat

Peace is the sea. I can see
a boat slowly bobbing along.

Peace is a baby sleeping
as quietly as a mouse.

Peace is a church bell ringing
Ding-a-ling-a-ling

Peace is reading a book,
Slowly saying the words.

Peace is the postman
Bringing me letters.

Peace is a flag
Fluttering in the wind.

Peace is a squirrel
Collecting nuts

Peace is a beetle
Scurrying along.

Henry Crowther, Year 4

A Mother's Prayer

Where are they now,
The children lost in war?
Those looks of mute and hopeless horror
Have no business with little faces
Made for cheeky grins in happy places.

Dear God, do not welcome them with splendour.
Heavenly choirs are not required.
Is there, perhaps, a plumper angel,
Ample bosomed, patient, kind,
Who likes games, can bake cakes
And has a loving smile?

And dear God, in your infinite mercy,
Remember, oh remember please,
A teddy and a blanket,
A tickle and a tease.

Sue Hunt

A Peace Dividend

Steps up the path. A knock on the door.

He'd been away at the war, at the war.

He'd no key, which was why he knocked on the door.

A long time away, in years more than four.

Who would be there to answer the door?

A little boy nervously went to the door,

Lifted the latch and blinked as he saw

A tall scary stranger; not seen him before.

"Hey mum, please come quick. A strange man at the door."

She came running pale. She had not expected

Her husband so soon and sadly reflected

"We'd not heard you were coming. Why didn't you write?"

"I hoped to surprise you," he said. But the sight

Of a child at Mum's apron just didn't seem right.

"Whose, child is this?" the husband then cried.

"He's yours, your own special son," she replied.

"Who's he?" asked the boy. "He's your dad," his mum said.

"But mum," said the boy. "You thought he was dead".

Like so many soldiers just back from the war

It took time to forgive a small son at the door.

Now there was peace they all had to try

To build a new world and find love thereby.

George Metcalfe, Mayor of Canterbury

Peace is...

Cuddling up in bed on a quiet night

or

Playing on my tablet on the sofa.

Being with my family

or

Reading a good book in bed.

Swimming in the pool on holiday

or

Practising penalties in the garden.

Drawing a picture with my Dad at the table

and

Knowing there's tasty pizza for tea.

Alex Richardson - Year 4

14 Descriptions of Peace

Peace is a busy classroom and graffitied textbooks
the shrill call of the bell disturbing a lesson
the sudden scraping of chairs and raising of voices
announcing the start of break time.

Peace is sharp pencils and colouring pens
it's bubble writing on sugar paper
folded notes about who fancies who
it's fingers sticky from tubs of snow-white glue.

Peace is fighting over which toy to play with
a screaming playground of kiss-chase
intense 10-minute football matches
cries of "tag" over the furious thundering of feet.

Peace is a half-finished football sticker album
and the dread of not getting that last shiny
it's well-arranged collections of stuff
and scrapbooks full of keepsakes.

Peace is racing a bike too fast

through landscaped trees and green spaces

it's scraped knees and blue plasters

it's dusting yourself down and doing it again.

Peace is that moment of almost silence

after an orchestra has tuned up, but before the song begins

and you play your instrument

becoming a small part of something much bigger.

Peace is a brightly-coloured cartoon series blaring from the TV

it's silly voices and outrageous characters

villains who contribute to their own demise

where the good guys usually win.

Peace is pretending to be a time-travelling dinosaur

with your trusty plasma sword in hand

on a quest to rescue the galactic Prince

from the evil forces of doom's legions.

Peace is a hot bath and a good scrub

time to soak your skin and warm the muscles

having the space to breathe slowly

and draw pictures in the mirror's condensation.

Peace is the sun setting in a darkening sky

a stretched out evening of watching stars

it's building a fire and turning marshmallows on
sticks

telling scary stories, knowing that, really, you're
safe.

Dan Simpson

The Friendship Bench

Every colour
    and every creed,
People with money
    and people in need.
We want
everyone sitting on the friendship bench.

Football fans
    from rival teams.
"Beat you next time."
    "In your dreams."

We want mums and dads
    who can't get along,
brothers and sisters
    always in the wrong.
We want
everyone sitting on the friendship bench.

We want families crying,
    Squabbling, bickering,
noisy neighbours
    tempers quickening.

Overloud voices
    sounding out,
pressure groups shouting,
    what they're about,
everyone sitting on the friendship bench.

We want criminals, judges,
    Prisoners and jailers,
Bullies and victims,
    thieves, blackmailers,
everyone sitting on the friendship bench.

No need to argue,
    no need to fight,
nobody thinking that
    might is right,
just
everyone sitting on the friendship bench.

We want positive, negative,

> black and white,

darkness giving way

> to the light.

We want hope for the future,

> Lessons from the past,

the sort of friendship

> that lasts and lasts.

we want

everyone sitting on the friendship bench.

We want aggravation,

> assimilation,

recrimination,

> United Nations,

everyone sitting on the friendship bench.

From the naughty corner
    to the friendship bench,
everyone sitting on the friendship bench
everyone sitting on the friendship bench
everyone sitting on the friendship bench.

So go on, say who
    you'd like to see,
on the friendship bench
    sitting peacefully
with you
and
me.

Brian Moses

taken from 'Lost Magic: The Very Best of Brian Moses' (Macmillan, September 2016)

Cousins

Every evening

when the dark creeps in

like a smothering black cape,

our little family

- Mum, Dad, Brother, Sister, Gogo the cat and me –

we get together to huddle and cuddle

and keep us each safe.

Every night

when the moon rises like a white saucer,

our little family

- Mum, Dad, Brother, Sister, Gogo the cat and me –

go to bed in our warm rooms.

We tuck each other in

and sleep safe in green dreams.

But in another land,

when the same dark creeps in,

a broken family in a wild wind

looks to the same moon, red and angry,

and each makes a wish,

- Mum, Dad, Brother, Sister, Asmara the stray dog –

all ask for food, for medicine, for peace, for rain.

Just these, only these, do our beautiful cousins ask for.

John Rice

Fascinating Facts

The ibis, a blue bird was a symbol of Thoth, the God of wisdom and learning. Thoth mediated between good and evil in three epic battles and is associated with judgement.

"There'll be bluebirds over the white cliffs of Dover" was a popular song in World War II sung by Vera Lynn. The song claimed that when the war was over bluebirds would fly over the white cliffs of Dover. In reality bluebirds are not found in Europe but are native to North America.

The Battle of Agincourt took place between the English and the French in 1415 during the Hundred Years War, a series of conflicts fought over the succession to the French throne. Sadly the war did not end until 1453, 38 years after the battle.

The Second Punic War between Carthage and the Roman Republic lasted from 218 to 210 BCE. Its end in 210 BCE heralded 50 years of peace. The Carthaginians had a cavalry of elephants whilst the Romans used javelin throwers as part of their army.

The Treaty of Kadesh was the world's earliest peace treaty. It was signed by Ramesses II and Hattusilis III in 1259 BC to end the war between the Egyptians and the Hittites which had lasted over two centuries. It promised "brotherhood and peace forever." Sadly it did not bring the peace it promised.

Hot air balloons have been used in time of war. Barrage balloons, known as 'blimps' were used by the British during world war II to intercept air attacks by German bombers.

The Christmas Truce of 1914 was a series of widespread but unofficial ceasefires during the First World War. Soldiers on both sides exchanged presents, sang carols and played football.

St Francis of Assisi is the patron saint of animals. One day he met a boy carrying a basket of wild doves to sell at market. He felt sad to see the beautiful birds imprisoned and asked the boy if he could have the basket. Francis released the birds, who then perched on his shoulder and he called them the 'Little Sisters'. The white dove is the symbol of peace.

The Children's Society was founded in 1881 when Edward Rudolf, a Sunday school teacher discovered two of his pupils begging for food on the streets. The boys' father had died, leaving their mother to raise 7 children under the age of 11. Today the charity works with vulnerable children across the UK.

Activity

Could you write a poem about peace? Think of a place that is special to you, or where you feel safe.